Picture credits:

t=top b=bottom m=middle l=left r=right c=centre

U.S. Geological Survey (USGS): 11bl, 21tl, 25m, 28bl, 29t, 30m, 31tl, 31b, 33l, 33m, 34bl, 34m, 38b, 43tl

D.A. Swanson/U.S. Geological Survey (USGS): 7t

R.L. Christiansen/U.S. Geological Survey (USGS): 9tm, 23br

C. Stoughton/U.S. Geological Survey (USGS): 10tr

J.D. Griggs/D.A. Swanson/U.S. Geological Survey (USGS): 21m

D.W. Peterson/U.S. Geological Survey (USGS): 23m

R.L. Christiansen/J.D. Griggs/U.S. Geological Survey (USGS): 25br

J.D. Griggs/U.S. Geological Survey (USGS): 24bl

Austin Post/U.S. Geological Survey (USGS): 26tr

D.W. Peterson/R.L. Christiansen/U.S. Geological Survey (USGS): 26bl

R.T. Holcomb/D.A. Swanson/U.S. Geological Survey (USGS): 42bl

Office of Oceanic and Atmospheric Research (OAR)/National Undersea Research Program (NURP): 12tr, 14bl, 24tr

National Aeronautics and Space Administration (NASA): 18tr, 19t, 19b, 42br

Commander John Bortniak/
National Oceanic and Atmospheric Administration (NOAA): 13m

Digital Globe: 35t, 35br

Published By: Robert Frederick Ltd.
4 North Parade Bath, England.
First Published: 2005

Designed and packaged by
Q2A Creative
Printed in China

VOLCANOES & EARTHQUAKES

CONTENTS

Inside the Earth

The ground under your feet may feel all strong and firm, but the Earth's inside is far from that. The topmost covering of the Earth is called the crust. The crust has three layers under it: the mantle, the outer core and the inner core. The crust and the upper mantle make up the lithosphere.

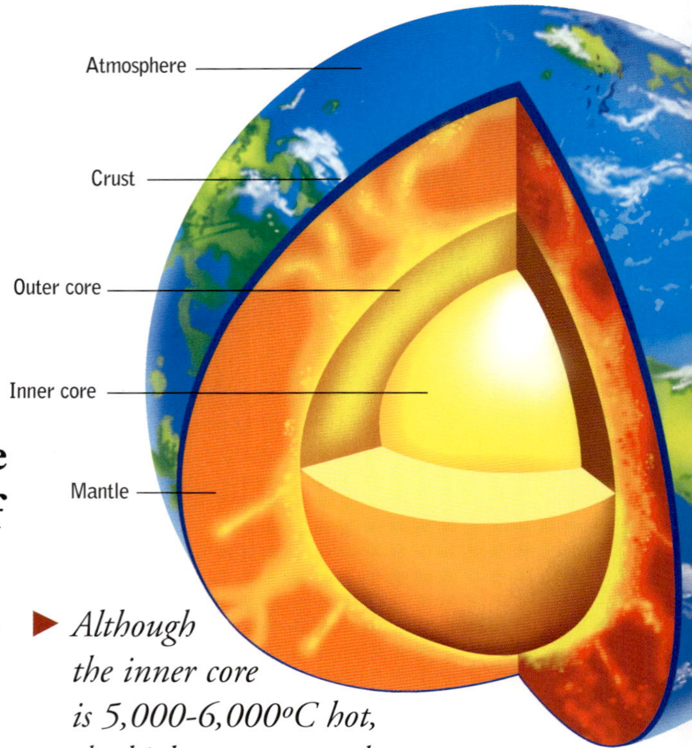

▶ *Although the inner core is 5,000-6,000ºC hot, the high pressures make sure the core is in solid form*

Hot as the Sun

The mantle is a thick layer of rock below the crust and is made up of silicon, oxygen, aluminium, iron and magnesium. Next comes the outer core, which is in molten liquid form. At the centre of the Earth is the inner core and it is believed to be as hot as the Sun!

▼ *As the tectonic plates on the Earth's crust move, they often hit each other at the edges. Here the plates are sliding past each other*

▲ *When tectonic plates strike against each other, one plate usually pushes under the other one*

Like a football

Just as a football has many joints on its surface, the Earth's crust is also made of rocky plates placed next to each other. These are called tectonic plates. But unlike a football, these plates are not joined and often collide with each other.

Getting shaky

Most earthquakes occur along the boundaries of the rocky plates. These plates collide against each other, causing the Earth to shake – either mildly or really hard!

INTERESTING FACT

The upper part of the mantle has a temperature of about 870°C. This temperature gradually increases down through the mantle to about 2200°C near the outer core. At the core the temperature may be as high as 7000°C.

FACT FILE

DEPTH FROM EARTH'S SURFACE

- **Mantle:** Up to 2,900 km (1,802 miles)
- **Outer core:** Up to 5,150 km (3,200 miles)
- **Inner core:** Up to 6,400 km (3,977 miles)

Throwing up fire

When the Earth spews out melted rock from deep within, it leads to volcanoes. Volcanoes are openings on the Earth's surface through which lava, hot gases and rock fragments erupt.

▲ *Volcanic eruptions throw up three kinds of materials: lava, rocks and gases*

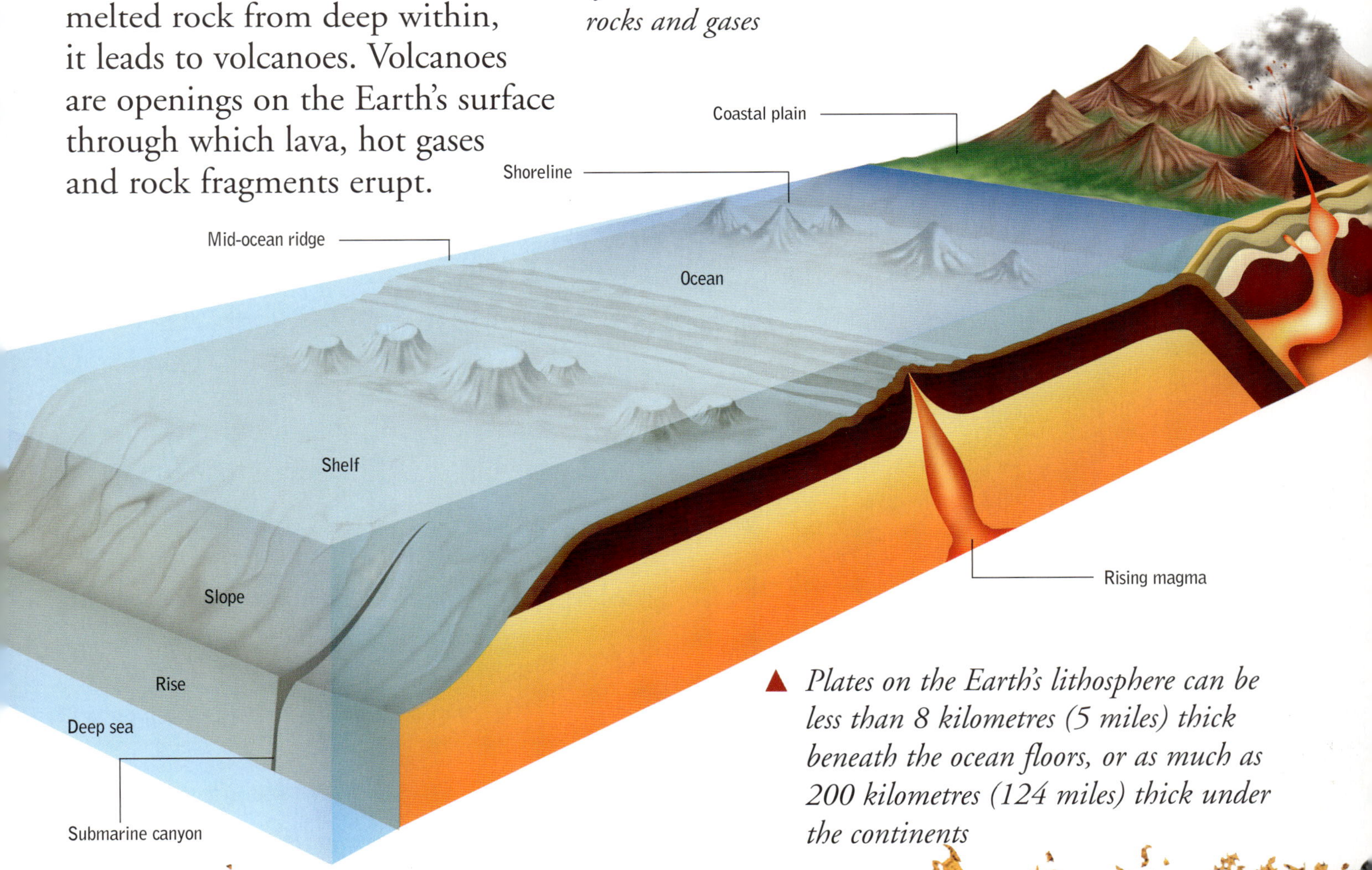

▲ *Plates on the Earth's lithosphere can be less than 8 kilometres (5 miles) thick beneath the ocean floors, or as much as 200 kilometres (124 miles) thick under the continents*

Volcanoes

An erupting volcano is perhaps one of the most spectacular sights on Earth. Volcanoes are like nature's own fireworks – but these are much more powerful and dangerous. A violent eruption can blow apart an entire mountain.

► *Most volcanoes erupt with enormous force, throwing lava, fireballs and ash high into the air*

Awesome power

Powerful activities within the Earth cause volcanoes. An opening on the Earth's surface is formed, through which lava, hot gases and rock fragments spew out.

◄ *The volcanic materials gradually pile up around the vent, forming a volcanic mountain, or volcano*

Melting magma

Extreme heat inside the Earth melts the rocks to form magma and gas. The gas-filled magma slowly rises toward the Earth's surface from the mantle. As more magma rises, it forms a large chamber near to the surface.

▲ *Hotspots are regions inside the Earth that are believed to be very hot. Some types of volcanoes, like those in Hawaii, are formed over hotspots. Scientists have yet to completely understand all about hotspots*

Venting out

From the chamber the magma melts a channel, or conduit, to rise up to the surface. Conduits are formed in weaker areas of the Earth's surface. As the magma approaches the surface, it blasts out through an opening called the central vent.

INTERESTING FACT

Some eruptions occur on volcanic islands. These islands are the peaks of volcanic mountains rising up from the ocean floor. Such mountains are built by repeated eruptions over a period of time. There are other eruptions that occur along narrow cracks in the ocean floor. In this case, the lava flows away from the cracks and helps build up the sea bottom – or ends up creating a future mountain.

FACT FILE

- Most magma forms at 80 to 160 km (50 to 99 miles) beneath the surface
- Magma chambers form about 3 km (1.9 miles) below Earth's surface
- Magma is estimated to be as hot as 1,000-1,200°C
- Lava is as hot as 900-1,170°C

▼ *Volcanic eruptions in the ocean deposit large amounts of lava on the ocean floor, and over time this builds above sea level and forms an island*

Spitting fire

In some eruptions, huge fiery clouds rise over the mountain, and glowing streams of lava flow down its sides. In others, red-hot ash and cinders shoot out of the mountaintop, and large lumps of hot rock are thrown out high into the air.

Volcano Classification

Not all volcanoes are alike and scientists divide them in many ways – depending on how often they erupt, their shape, the kind of molten rock they are made of, and more.

On and off

Active volcanoes are those that either erupt constantly or have erupted in recent times. Although generally quiet, they can be violent at times. Intermittent volcanoes erupt at regular periods, while dormant volcanoes are the sleeping ones – they have become inactive for a while, but an eruption is possible again. Extinct volcanoes have been inactive during recorded history. They probably will never erupt again

▲ *Lava eruption at Kilauea Iki, a crater situated east of the active Kilauea volcano in the Hawaii Island*

◀ *Mt Kilimanjaro is a dormant, snow-capped volcano. Located in Tanzania, it is the highest mountain in Africa*

Free-flowing

Shield volcanoes are formed when a large amount of free-flowing lava spills from a vent and spreads widely. The lava slowly builds up a low, broad and dome-shaped mountain. Thousands of separate, overlapping lava streams – each less than 15 metres (49 feet) thick – formed Mauna Loa in the Hawaii Island, U.S.

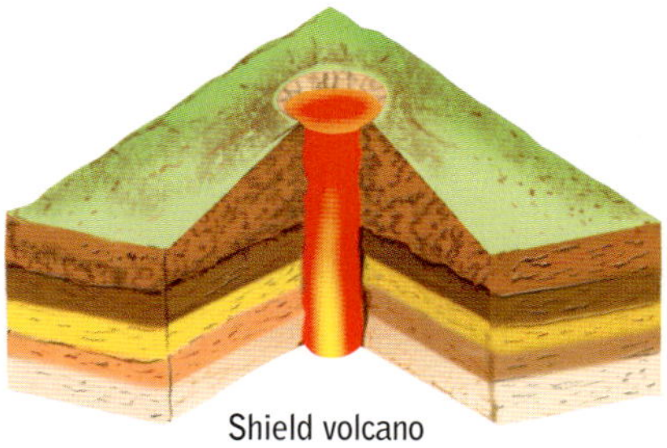

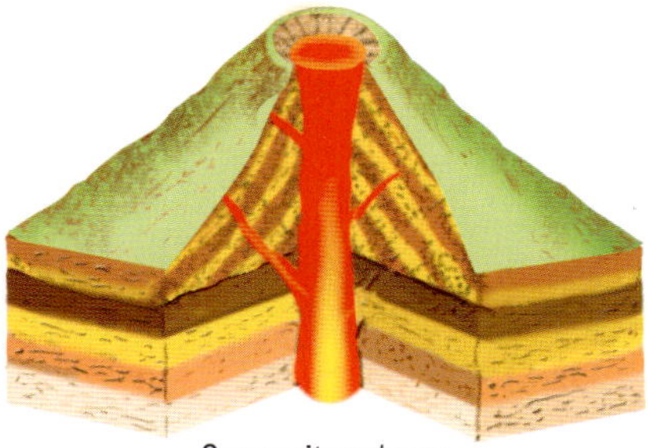

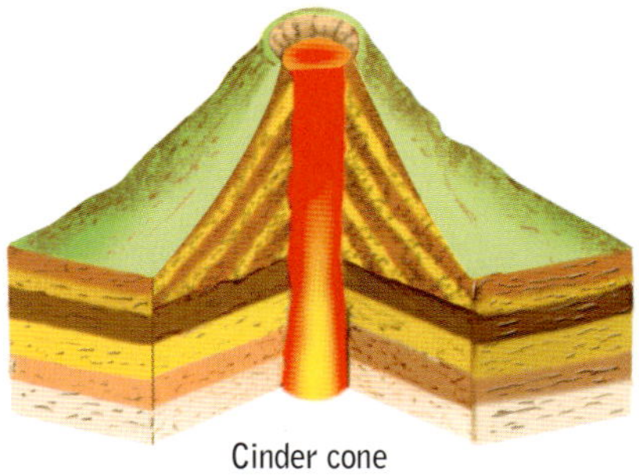

▲ *Among the prominent types of volcanic landforms are shield volcanoes, cinder cones and composite volcanoes*

Layered on

Composite volcanoes are formed when both lava and rock fragments erupt from a central vent. These materials pile up in alternate layers around the vent. Several such layers build up into a towering – and usually cone-shaped – mountain.

◀ *Lassen Volcanic National Park at the Cascade Range in northern California, U.S., features the Lassen volcanic peak. The volcano erupted last in 1921*

INTERESTING FACT

Parícutin in Mexico is a famous cinder cone. It began in 1943, when a crack opened in the ground on a farmer's field. When the eruptions ended in 1952, the top of the cone was 2,808 metres (9,210 feet) from the base.

FACT FILE

- **Shield:** Mauna Loa, Hawaii Island
- **Cinder cone:** Parícutin, west-central Mexico
- **Composite:** Mt Fuji, Japan; Vesuvius, Italy
- **Active:** Stromboli, off the coast of Italy; Mt Asama, Japan; Mt Etna, Sicily
- **Intermittent:** Hualalai, Hawaii Island
- **Dormant:** Lassen Peak, California
- **Dead:** Aconcagua in Argentina and Mt Kenya in central Kenya

Conically inclined

Cinder cones build up when mostly rocky material erupts and falls back to gather around the vent. The accumulated material – mostly cinders – forms a cone-shaped mountain with a bowl-shaped crater at the top. The height can vary from a few metres to several hundreds of metres.

Volcanoes Under Sea

▲ *Pillow lava is formed when molten rock comes into contact with cold seawater or when eruptions occur in the sea*

Most volcanic eruptions occur on ocean floors. These submarine eruptions occur along narrow cracks in the ocean floor. The lava flows away from the cracks, building up the sea bottom or the sea crust. However, nobody has yet observed a deep submarine eruption live.

Invisible

Since most submarine eruptions occur in the deep, one cannot see them from the surface. Only special features formed by the volcanic action have been observed. Submarine volcanoes can lead to island formation, as the erupted lava and volcanic matter accumulate over the years.

Cool and solid

The high pressure exerted by the water makes oceanic volcanoes behave differently from the ones situated on land. The pressure keeps the gases and steam in solution, preventing any violent explosion. In the usual course, the lava flows down the slopes quietly in blocks, spreading out in a pillow-like manner. The lava cools down quickly to become solid, and tends to collect along the sides of the slope.

◀ *The mid-ocean ridge system encircles the Earth like the seams of a baseball. The Earth's crust on these seams is continually moving apart, creating new ocean floor. The ridges have thousands of individual volcanoes that erupt periodically*

Sand and rubble

Lava erupting from volcanoes on a shallow sea floor, or flowing into the sea from land, cools very rapidly. This splits the lava into sand and rubble, which may get deposited on the coastal areas, as in the case of the famous 'black sand' beaches of Hawaii.

▼ *The black sand beaches of Hawaii were created by the violent interaction between hot lava and seawater*

Shallow waters

When volcanoes erupt in shallow waters, they can blast steam and rock debris high above the sea surface. The ocean currents can cause the debris to drift over a large area. Most debris usually gets deposited on the sea floor, though.

INTERESTING FACT

Although toxic to most living organisms, some exotic and specially adapted life forms live near the vents of submarine volcanoes. The lava creates the edges of new oceanic plates and also helps in producing heat and chemicals that support certain living organisms.

FACT FILE

- **Numbers:** Estimated at over a million worldwide
- **Average depth:** About 2,600 metres (8,500 feet)
- **Mid-ocean ridges produce:** About 75 per cent of the magma worldwide

◀ *Chimney-like structures called 'black smokers' form when hot water flows out through volcanic lava on a mid-ocean ridge*

▶ *Tubeworms, some up to 1.5 metres (5 feet) long, cluster around hot springs on the ocean floor*

Rocks and Minerals

▼ *The violet-coloured amethyst is a form of the mineral quartz and is prized as a gem*

Three kinds of materials can erupt from a volcano. These include lava, rock fragments and gas. The material that comes out of volcanoes depends chiefly on how sticky or fluid the magma is.

Red-hot

Lava is the name for magma that has escaped on to the Earth's surface. When lava reaches the surface, it is extremely hot. Then, as it starts to cool down, the lava hardens into different kinds of matter.

Rocky matter

Igneous rocks such as basalt are formed as lava cools above the ground. Such rocks are also created when the magma gets trapped in small pockets inside the Earth. These cool off slowly to form igneous rocks like granite.

◀ *The ocean floor is mostly made up of basalt, which is formed by lava flowing from cracks in the mid-ocean ridge*

Mineral mine

Most of the metallic minerals mined in the world – such as copper, gold, silver, lead and zinc – are a result of volcanic activities over the years. These minerals are found in magma deep in the roots of extinct volcanoes, and are mined from there.

Blasting tephra

Rock fragments called tephra originate in sticky magma. Since the magma is sticky, it does not allow the gas to escape. The trapped gas builds up so much pressure that it blasts the magma into fragments. Tephra includes volcanic dust, volcanic ash and volcanic bombs.

INTERESTING FACT

Volcanic dust can be carried large distances. In 1883, the eruption of Krakatoa in Indonesia sent dust some 27 kilometres (17 miles) up into the air. The dust flew around the Earth several times and produced luminous red sunsets in many parts of the world.

FACT FILE

- **Lava temperature:** More than 1,100°C
- **Volcanic dust:** Diameter less than 0.25 millimetre
- **Volcanic ash:** Diameter less than 0.5 centimetre
- **Volcanic bomb:** Diameter over 64 millimetres (2.5 inches)

◄ *Diamonds are brought to the surface from the mantle in an unusual type of magma called kimberlite, which erupts at a type of volcanic vent called a diatreme or pipe*

▼ *Pumice rocks are igneous rocks formed when the lava cools quickly above the ground. The rocks are very light and have pores on them*

Geysers and Hot Springs

Apart from erupting vents, the areas around volcanoes have other interesting features as well. These include hot springs and water geysers. Mud pots are formed when the heated water is mixed with mud and clay over the vent. The gases trying to escape through the vent causes the mud pot to bubble. And if the hot water reaches the surface only in the form of steam, it is called a fumarole.

▲ *The water in hot springs often boils to give off steam. One can even see bubbles on the surface. The Crested Pool at Yellowstone National Park, U.S., is one such hot spring*

▼ *People believe minerals in hot springs are helpful for health. Many take baths in them to treat rheumatism and other ailments*

Hot springs

Hot springs are gushes of hot water that are found on the land surface. These are formed when molten materials deep in the Earth cool down, giving off water vapour. The hot vapour moves up through cracks in the rocks, cooling down in the process. Gradually it condenses to become water and pours forth from the ground.

▶ *Geysers usually discharge hot water and steam up to heights of 50 metres (164 feet), but can at times even reach 500 metres (1,640 feet)*

Rich in mineral

The water from hot springs is clear and rich in mineral content. The minerals are dissolved from the rocks as these move from under the Earth. Countries such as Japan, New Zealand, Kenya and Iceland are well-known for hot springs.

Natural fountains

Geysers are nature's own fountains of water wherein a vent at the surface throws up jets of hot water and steam. Scientists believe these are created when water enters cavities inside the Earth's surface and interacts with rock heated by magma.

INTERESTING FACT

Geysers and hot springs are formed from submarine volcanoes as well. Water percolates down through cracks in the rocks in the mid-ocean ridge, moving towards the sea floor. There the water is superheated before gushing out from vents at temperatures of some 300°C to 400°C.

FACT FILE

- **Highest geyser at present**
  Steamboat Geyser,
  at Norris Geyser Basin,
  Yellowstone National Park, U.S.
  Height: 116 metres (380 feet)
- **Highest ever**
  Waimangu Geyser,
  New Zealand, before it was
  wiped out by landslides in 1904
  Height: Over 300 metres
  (1,000 feet)

Shooting up

The heat from the molten rocks boils the water and the high pressure builds up bubbles of steam. Finally, the pressure is strong enough to shoot out the water and steam upwards through a vent. This cycle can be repeated regularly.

◄ *Fumaroles are weak geysers that vent out volcanic gases, such as sulphur vapour, from fissures*

Extraterrestrial Volcanoes

Earth is not the only place where volcanoes occur. Scientists have observed proof of volcanic activities on the Earth's Moon and other planets of the solar system. Volcanoes on the Moon and planets such as Mars and Venus are nearly three to four billion years old.

Sea of lava

The Earth's Moon has no large volcanoes like the Hawaiian ones or Mount St Helens in the United States. However, vast parts of the lunar surface are covered with lava. The earliest astronomers mistook these to be water and called them 'mare' (Latin for 'sea').

Galileo was an unmanned spacecraft sent by NASA to study the planet Jupiter and its moons. The Galileo probe images revealed active volcanoes on Jupiter's moon Io

Quiet flow

There are no violent volcanic eruptions on the Moon due to the lack of dissolved water and lack of gravity. The lunar mare shows some small volcanic domes and cones, but these are largely flat and comprise broad, slim layers around the vent. Since the Moon's gravity is less than Earth's, the lava is more fluid and flows out easily and quietly over large areas.

◀ *The largest volcano on Mars, Olympus Mons, is a circular structure that would span the entire Hawaiian island chain on Earth!*

MARS

Largest shield volcanoes

Mars has the largest shield volcanoes in the solar system, though the numbers are few. The 'red planet' also has large volcanic cones, mare-like volcanic plains and other smaller features. However, there are hardly any active volcanoes on Mars today.

INTERESTING FACT

The innermost large moon of Jupiter, called Io, is literally bursting with volcanoes. It is the most volcanically active body known in the solar system. The volcanoes there are the hottest spots in the solar system, with temperatures exceeding 1,527°C.

FACT FILE

VOLCANOES ON MARS

- **Numbers:** Less than 20; only 5 of these are giant shields
- **Largest:** Olympus Mons, 550 km (340 miles) in diameter and 2 km (15 miles) high

VOLCANOES ON VENUS

- **Numbers:** About 1,600 major volcanoes
- Average size of **shield volcanoes** 100-600 km (62-373 miles) across, heights 0.3-5 km (0.2-3 miles)

Most numbers

Venus has more volcanoes than any other planet in the solar system. No one can be sure about how many there are, and the total can be even over a million. Most volcanoes on Venus are shield volcanoes, but there are some unusual ones as well. Again, it cannot be proved for certain that the volcanoes are no longer active.

▼ *Volcano eruptions on Venus involve fluid lava flows. There is no sign of explosive, ash-forming eruptions*

Famous Volcanoes

There are more than 500 active volcanoes on Earth's surface. These are known to have erupted at least once in recorded history and some of these have gained fame for various reasons.

When Vesuvius erupted in AD 79, the column of ash rose up to nearly two kilometres. The eruption lasted 19 hours, and killed more than 10,000 people

In 1748, a peasant chanced upon a brick wall, and excavations of Pompeii began. About three-quarters of Pompeii has now been uncovered. Visitors can see buildings as they stood almost 2,000 years ago

Vesuvius

Mt Vesuvius is a volcano east of Naples, Italy. One of the most violent explosions on Vesuvius occurred in AD 79, completely destroying the ancient Roman cities of Pompeii and Herculaneum. It has erupted many times since then and is regarded as one of the most dangerous volcanoes in the world.

▲ *The violent eruption of Mount St Helens in 1980 blew the top of the mountain off, reducing its summit by 400 metres (1,312 feet) and replacing it with a horseshoe-shaped crater*

INTERESTING FACT

In AD 79, Mt Vesuvius was thought to be extinct – its crater being covered with vegetation. As a result, its eruption took the cities by surprise. Pompeii and Herculaneum were so thoroughly covered that ruins of the cities remained uncovered for nearly 1,700 years.

FACT FILE

- **Mt Etna:** Highest summit over 3,200 metres (10,000 feet) high; base of about 150 km (93 miles)
- **Mt St Helens:** About 2,550 metres (8,363 feet) high
- **Mt Vesuvius cone:** Currently 1,281 metres (4,203 feet) high
- **Mauna Loa:** About 4,170 metres (13,681 feet) high

St Helens

Mount St Helens is an active volcano in Washington, U.S. The first recorded eruption was in 1800, while the most devastating one took place in 1980. The latter killed 57 people and thousands of animals, and destroyed over 200 homes. The eruption lasted over nine hours.

◄ *Mauna Loa is among the most active volcanoes on Earth. It has erupted 33 times since its first recorded eruption in 1843. The most recent one was in 1984*

Mauna Loa

Mauna Loa is the largest active volcano on Earth and makes up nearly half of Hawaii Island. It is an active shield volcano that erupted last in 1984. In Hawaiian, 'mauna loa' means 'long mountain'.

Mount Etna

Mount Etna is an active volcano on the east coast of Sicily. It is the highest volcano in Europe and has the longest history of recorded eruptions.

More Famous Volcanoes

▼ *For generations, Mt Rainier was known as Takhoma or Tahoma. But on May 8, 1792, Captain George Vancouver of the British Royal Navy officially named it after his friend, Rear Admiral Peter Rainier!*

Volcanoes inspire feelings of awe in perhaps everyone. But there is more to the phenomenon than just fire and fury, or lava and ash. That is the reason why volcanoes have been an object of curiosity and interest among both scientists and common people.

▼ *The famous cone-shaped, active Mt Fuji volcano in Japan remains completely buried in snow in the winter*

Mt Fuji

Mount Fuji is the highest mountain in Japan. Surrounded by the Five Lakes, it is also one of the most scenic of all volcanoes. The volcano is designated as active, though with low risk of eruption. The last recorded eruption occurred in 1707.

Stromboli

Stromboli has one of the longest recorded periods of activity. It is a small island in the Tyrrhenian Sea, Italy. For at least the last 2,000 years, it has erupted almost regularly.

Mt Rainier

Mount Rainier is located in Pierce County, in Washington, U.S. Rainier is mostly covered by glaciers. It is a famous destination for winter sports, including snowshoeing and skiing. The most recent eruption was over 175 years ago.

Kilauea in the Hawaii Island is famed for its frequent eruptions, though most of these are confined within the crater. Some of its major violent explosions were recorded in 1955, 1975 and 1983

INTERESTING FACT

Indonesia has had the most active volcanoes in recorded time – as many as 76. These volcanoes have reported a total of 1,171 eruptions, which have caused a large number of fatalities.

FACT FILE

- **Mt Ranier:** Above 4,392 metres (14,410 feet)
- **Mt Fuji:** 3,776 metres (12,388 feet)
- **Stromboli:** 900 metres (2,900 feet)
- **Kilauea:** 1,222 metres (4,009 feet) at the summit

Lava flow from a volcanic eruption can travel for miles before it cools down and becomes solid. Everything that comes in the way of the hot lava gets knocked down or catches fire. But since the lava flows slowly, people can usually get out of its way in good time

Kilauea

Kilauea is one of the world's most active volcanoes, with lava flowing almost continuously. Eruptions at Kilauea happen both from the summit and along the lengthy east and southwest rift zones that extend to the sea.

Volcanology

The study of volcanoes is called volcanology, and the people who study the science are called volcano-logists. A volcanologist's job is exciting and adventurous. To become a volcanologist, one needs to study maths and science in high school, and geology in college or at university!

▲ *The HUGO underwater observatory monitors the Loihi submarine volcano, off Hawaii. The project, begun in 1997, aims to study underwater volcanism*

Predicting eruptions

A volcanologist's main job is to predict volcanic eruptions. Little can be done to stop property damage in the surrounding areas when a volcano explodes. But many lives can be saved if people are shifted to a safe place before the eruption begins.

▲ *Geologist measuring the height of a lava fountain at an eruption of the Kilauea volcano in 1983*

Instruments used

Volcanologists use different instruments to predict an eruption. A tiltmeter is used to measure the expansion of a volcano by estimating the rising or lowering of magma levels. A device called a seismograph helps in detecting earthquakes caused by magma. Thermometers check for temperature rise in the area, while gas detectors measure the quantity of gases.

◀ *Volcanologists use a special type of thermometer called a thermocouple for measuring the temperature of lava*

Dangerous mission

Volcanologists must follow strict safety measures since they may be required to work near erupting volcanoes. Observatories have been set up on the slopes or rims of several volcanoes, among them Mount Asama in Japan, Kilauea in Hawaii, and Vesuvius in Italy. The Alaska observatory keeps track of the 100 active volcanoes in the region.

▲ *The Hawaiian Volcano Observatory (HVO) is perched on the rim of the Kilauea caldera. It was set up in 1912*

INTERESTING FACT

Some volcanoes, such as those in Hawaii, are easier to predict due to certain indicators. Before such a volcano erupts, the surface expands slightly as magma collects in the magma chamber. As the magma travels up, several small earthquakes occur while the surrounding areas experience rising temperatures. Also, clouds of gas escape from the vent.

FACT FILE

MOST ACTIVE VOLCANOES

- **Etna, Italy:** About 3,500 years
- **Stromboli, Italy:** About 2,000 years
- **Yasur, Vanuatu:** About 800 years
- **Ambrym, Vanuatu:** Since 1774, when it was sighted by Captain Cook
- **Tinakula, Solomon Islands:** Reportedly since 1951

▼ *Volcanologists wear an outfit similar to a spacesuit, along with a helmet and gloves. The suit helps them survive the hot temperature near erupting volcanoes*

Death on duty

Maurice and Katia Krafft were famous volcanologists who studied and photographed erupting volcanoes all over the world. They were killed by a hot ash flow while photographing the eruption of Unzen in Japan in 1991.

Volcanoes and the Weather

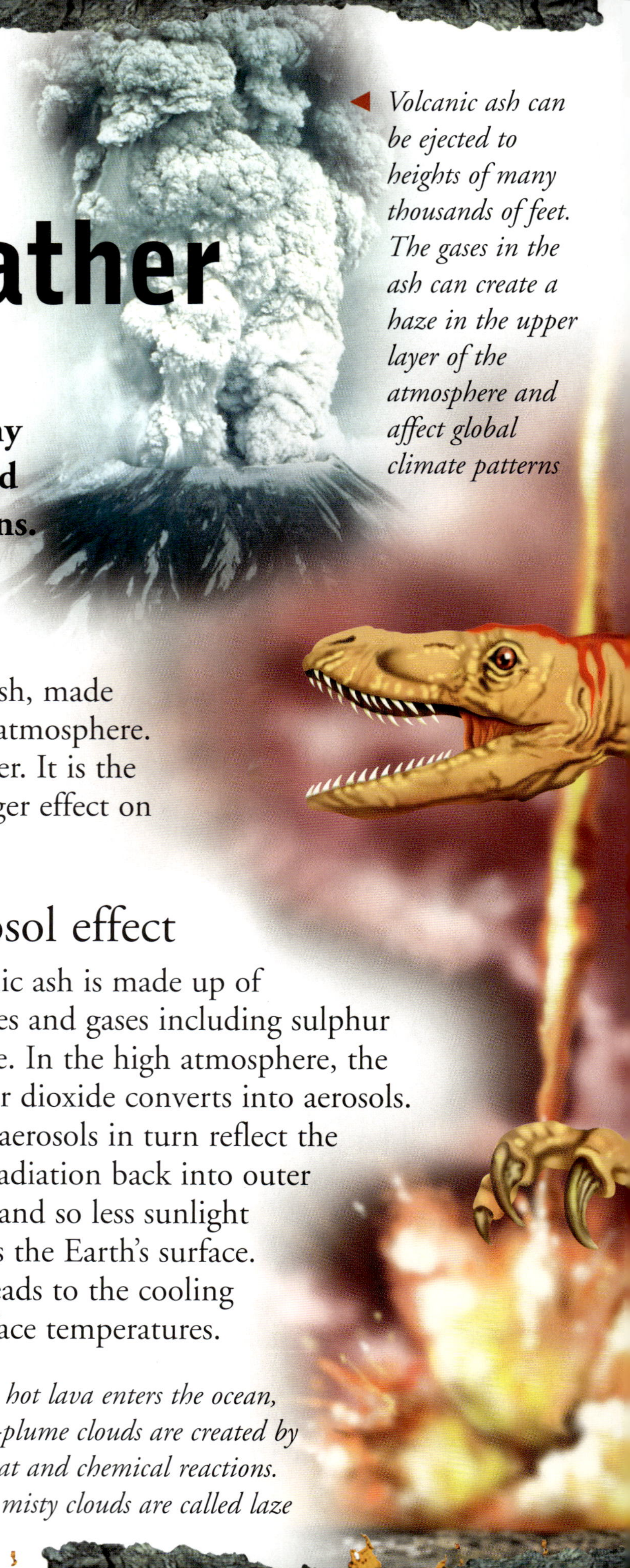

◀ *Volcanic ash can be ejected to heights of many thousands of feet. The gases in the ash can create a haze in the upper layer of the atmosphere and affect global climate patterns*

The Earth has witnessed gradual climatic changes over the years. Many factors have led to these changes, and one among them is volcanic eruptions.

Small outbursts

Minor eruptions take place around the world almost daily. In such cases volcanic ash, made up of rock and glass, is spun high into the atmosphere. But this has little or no effect on the weather. It is the large eruptions that are likely to have a bigger effect on the climate patterns of the Earth.

Aerosol effect

Volcanic ash is made up of particles and gases including sulphur dioxide. In the high atmosphere, the sulphur dioxide converts into aerosols. These aerosols in turn reflect the Sun's radiation back into outer space, and so less sunlight reaches the Earth's surface. This leads to the cooling of surface temperatures.

◀ *When hot lava enters the ocean, white-plume clouds are created by the heat and chemical reactions. These misty clouds are called laze*

When the Krakatoa erupted in 1883, the entire northern portion of the island was blown away

Krakatoa volcano

After the eruption of Krakatoa in Indonesia, in 1883, the volcanic dust was spread around the upper atmosphere by the jet streams. It is believed that world temperatures fell by an estimated 1.2°C.

INTERESTING FACT

The violent eruption of the Tambora volcano in Indonesia in 1815 led to the pollution of the atmosphere by a large quantity of volcanic dust. In addition to global temperatures falling by one degree Celsius, the following summer turned out to be unusually cold. In fact, the year 1816 came to be termed as "the year without a summer" in parts of Europe and North America.

FACT FILE

KRAKATOA ERUPTION

- Explosions heard over a third of the Earth's surface
- Ash thrown up as high as 80 kilometres (50 miles)
- Extent of material thrown out about 21 cubic kilometres (5 cubic miles)

Slowing down

Nonetheless, even the larger volcanic eruptions can only have a short-term effect on the Earth's climate, lasting perhaps a decade or so. Such eruptions will, at the most, only slow down the current trend of global warming rather than permanently halt it.

According to one theory, dinosaurs disappeared from the Earth due to volcanic eruptions. Over a period of several million years, volcanoes could have created enough dust and soot to block out sunlight. As a result, food became scarce and temperatures changed. Some scientists believe dinosaurs could not adapt and died out

Earthquakes

Various disturbances beneath the Earth's surface cause the ground to jolt or shake. This is called an earthquake. A strong earthquake can rattle many things, including buildings and bridges.

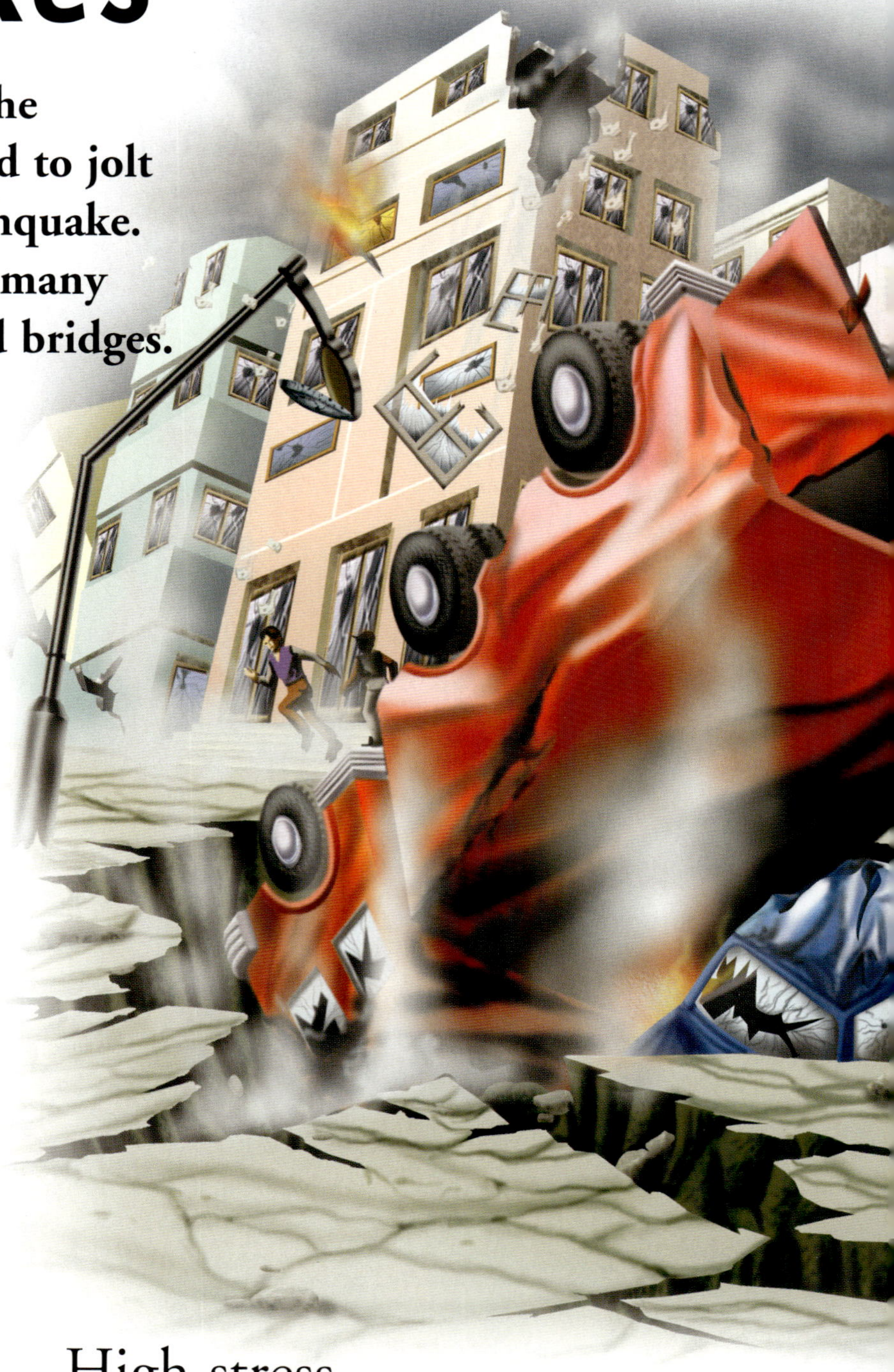

Faulty lines

Most earthquakes occur along a fault, which is a line or lines of fracture between blocks of rocks on the Earth's crust. As the tectonic plates move, they collide, move apart, or slide past one another, often causing faults. The presence of faults allows the rocks to shift relative to each other – one of the major factors behind earthquakes.

▼ *The San Andreas Fault in California is the point where the Pacific Plate and the North American Plate move against each other*

High stress

Over a period of time, built-up stress within the Earth causes large blocks of rock along a fault to strain, or bend. When the stress becomes too much, the resultant sudden release of energy by the rocks causes an earthquake.

Depending on the force of the ground motions, earthquakes can cause much damage to manmade structures like buildings, railways, bridges and dams

Primary focus

The point within the Earth where the rocks first break or shift is called the focus or hypocentre of the quake. The focus of most earthquakes lies within 70 kilometres (43 miles) beneath the surface, though the deepest can be at 700 kilometres (435 miles).

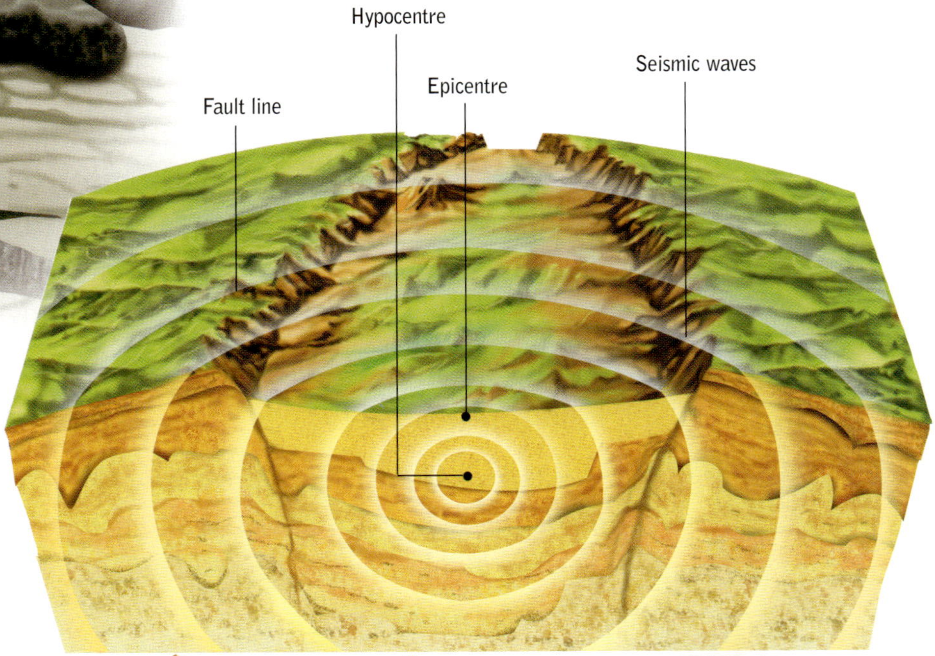

INTERESTING FACT

In an earthquake, the breaking of rock releases energy. This energy travels through the Earth in the form of seismic waves. The waves move out from the focus of an earthquake in all directions and become weaker as they get farther away.

FACT FILE

- At least 40 moderate earthquakes cause damage each year
- About one million small earthquakes occur annually, though these are too small to be felt
- On average, a powerful earthquake occurs less than once every two years
- The deepest earthquakes occur at depths of about 700 kilometres (435 miles)
- The most destructive earthquakes occur at depths within 70 kilometres (43 miles) of the Earth's surface

Epicentre

The point on the Earth's surface directly above the focus is the epicentre of the quake. The strongest shaking is usually felt near the epicentre.

The focus is the point of sudden movement inside the Earth wherein an earthquake occurs. The shock waves then travel towards the ground surface

Famous Earthquakes

Earthquakes almost never kill people directly. Rather, the deaths and injuries are caused due to the collapse of manmade structures like buildings, bridges and houses, or by fires resulting from broken gas and water lines. There is also danger from rockfalls and falling trees or tree branches.

Fire hazard

A major cause of death and property damage in earthquakes is fire. The 1906 San Francisco earthquake ranks as one of the worst disasters in American history because of a fire that raged for three days in the aftermath.

▲ *The California earthquake of April 18, 1906, lasted about 45 to 60 seconds, killing over 700 people*

Chilean quake

The Great Chilean Earthquake of May 22, 1960, is the largest earthquake in recorded history. The earthquake originated along the southern Chilean coast and caused a tsunami that hit Hawaii and the coastal areas of South America. About 3,000 people were killed in the earthquake/tsunami.

◄ *More than 90 per cent of the deaths during the 1964 earthquake in Alaska were due to the tsunamis that hit the coast after the shocks*

▲ *The Great Kanto Earthquake that shook Tokyo and Yokohama in Japan in 1923, left a trail of destructive fires*

Japan hit

The Great Kanto Earthquake in Japan, on September 1, 1923, caused huge destruction. Over one hundred thousand people were killed in the quake, which had a magnitude of 7.9 on the Richter scale. More than 88 fires broke out due to the quake.

INTERESTING FACT

After the Chilean earthquake in 1960, seismographs recorded seismic waves that travelled all around the Earth. These waves had the entire Earth in vibration for many days! The phenomenon is described as the 'free oscillation of the Earth'.

FACT FILE

MOST DEVASTATING

- **China, 1556:** Magnitude 8; over 830,000 dead
- **China, 1976:** Magnitude 7.8; over 270,000 dead
- **Syria, 1138:** Over 230,000 dead
- **China, 1927:** Magnitude 8.3; over 200,000 dead

▲ *The earthquake that struck San Fernando on February 9, 1971, ranks as one of the worst in the history of California. Measuring 6.5 on the Richter scale, the calamity caused the deaths of over 60 persons and extensive property damage*

Most deadly

The world's deadliest earthquake on record occurred in central China in 1556. Most people in the region lived in caves carved from soft rock. As the caves started to collapse during the earthquake, an estimated 830,000 people lost their lives.

Measuring Earthquakes

While an earthquake cannot be predicted accurately, scientists can measure its intensity. They can also accurately pin-point the epicentre and hypocentre of the earthquake.

▲ *Chinese philosopher Chang Hêng invented the earliest known seismoscope in AD 132. It resembled a wine jar with a six feet diameter. On the outside it had eight dragon heads facing the eight principal directions of the compass. During an earthquake, one of the dragon mouths would release a ball, depending on the direction of the shaking*

Richter scale

The most common instrument for measuring earthquake intensity is the Richter scale. It was developed in 1935 by seismologists Beno Gutenberg of Germany and Charles F. Richter of the United States. The scale is a series of numbers from 1 to 10, and each increase in number means an increase by a power of 10.

Increasing intensity

Every increase of one number in magnitude means the energy release of the quake is 32 times greater. For example, an earthquake of magnitude 7.0 releases 32 times more energy than an earthquake measuring 6.0.

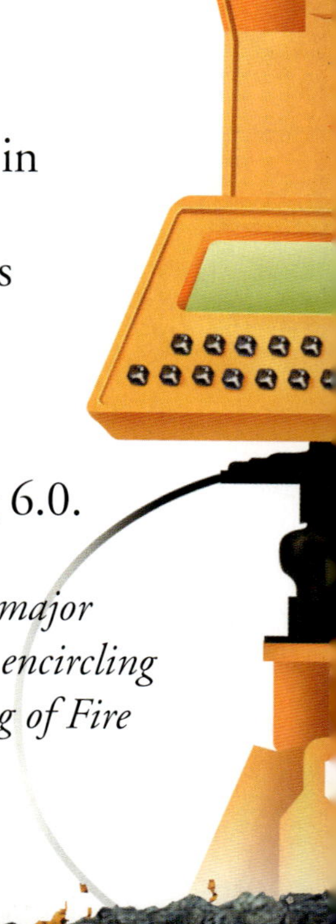

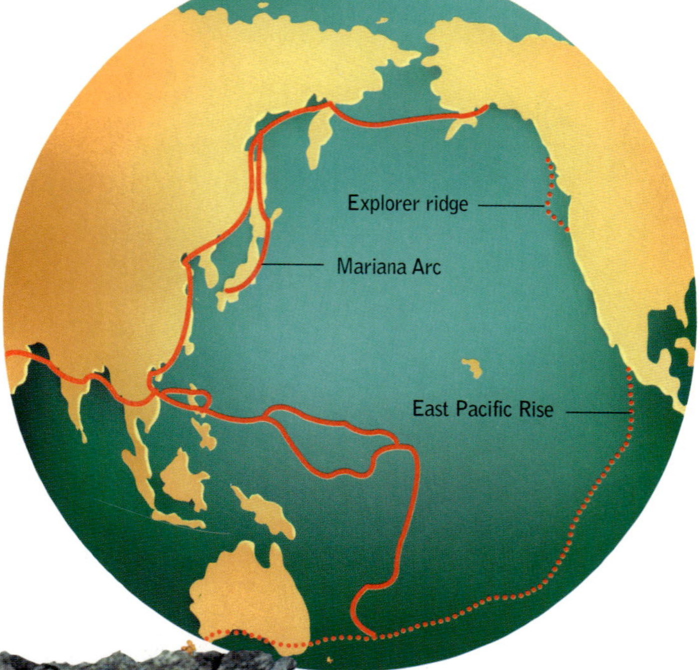

◀ *About 80 per cent of the world's major earthquakes happen along a belt encircling the Pacific Ocean, called the Ring of Fire*

Seismic measure

The strength and location of earthquakes are recorded using an instrument known as a seismograph. It has sensors called seismometers that can detect movements in the ground.

▼ *The instruments at Honolulu geophysical observatory monitor tidal levels at remote sites throughout the Pacific Basin. These are used to warn about tsunamis*

INTERESTING FACT

An earthquake measuring 2 on the Richter scale can hardly be felt. On the other hand, a quake with magnitude greater than 7.0 may destroy many buildings.

FACT FILE

TOP 5 EARTHQUAKES

- **Chile,** 1960, 9.5 on the Richter scale
- **Alaska,** 1964, 9.2 on the Richter scale
- **Alaska,** 1957, 9.1 on the Richter scale
- **Kamchatka,** 1952, 9.0 on the Richter scale
- **Northern Sumatra,** 2004, 9.0 on the Richter scale

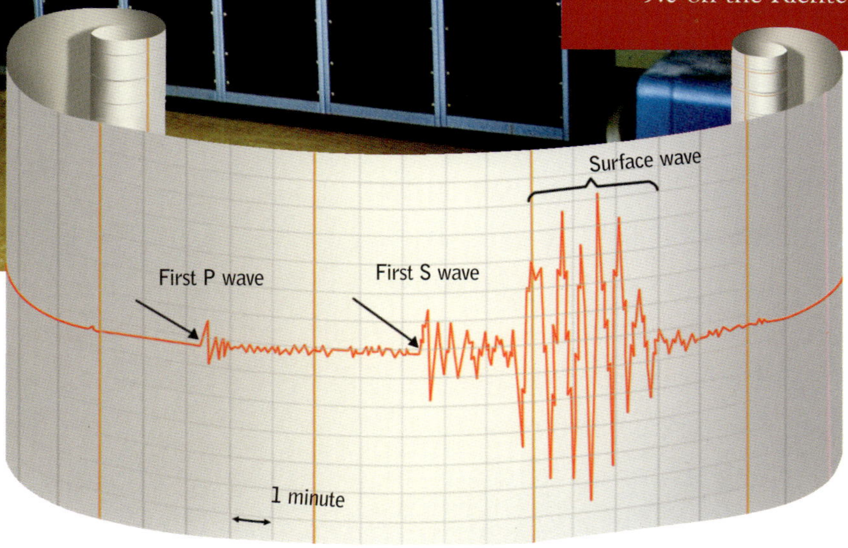

◀ *Scientists use the geodimeter to monitor changes on the Earth's surface near faults over a period of time. Thereby they hope to predict an earthquake with more accuracy*

▲ *The zigzag line made by a seismograph is called a seismogram. It shows the changing intensity of the vibrations from an earthquake*

Predictions

Scientists make long-term predictions of where earthquakes can occur. However, they are yet to develop a method to predict the exact time of an earthquake.

Features of Volcanoes and Earthquakes

Some earthquakes are caused by the movement of magma in volcanoes, and such quakes can be an early warning of volcanic eruptions. Earthquakes and volcanoes also give rise to phenomena like tsunamis, mudflows, ash flows and landslides.

Earthquakes can trigger landslides that cause loss of life and great damage to property

Flow of mud

Mudflows usually originate in volcanoes with large masses of ice and snow on their summits. They are caused by the speedy melting of a large amount of ice, caused by a volcanic eruption or due to an ice avalanche that has broken free because of an earthquake. These fast moving streams of mud sweep away anything in their path.

Tsunami crashes

Large earthquakes, and occasionally volcanic eruptions, beneath the ocean can create a series of huge, destructive waves called tsunamis that flood the coasts. Tsunamis gain in height when they reach shallow water near the shore.

Sometimes, volcanic ash combines with water in a stream and forms a boiling mudflow, which can be highly destructive

Before the tsunami hits the coast, the sea often recedes from the coast – like it did at the Kalutara Beach in Sri Lanka in 2004. If the slope is shallow, the withdrawal can exceed 800 metres (2,625 feet)

INTERESTING FACT

Although both are sea waves, a tsunami and a tidal wave are completely different. A tidal wave is a large sea wave generated by high winds, while a tsunami is a sea wave caused by an underwater disturbance (usually triggered by an earthquake) displacing the ocean water.

FACT FILE

- **Mudflow speed:** Nearly 100 km (62 miles) per hour on steep slopes
- **Tsunami height:** Up to 30 metres (98 feet)
- **Tsunami speed:** Average of 800 to 970 km (497 to 603 miles) per hour
- The term **'tsunami'** comes from the Japanese 'tsu' (harbour) and 'nami' (wave)

Indian Ocean

On December 26, 2004, an earthquake of magnitude 9.0 in the Indian Ocean triggered a series of killer tsunamis. At least 160,000 people were killed, making it the deadliest tsunami in recorded history.

The tsunamis of 2004 caused widespread destruction in Aceh in Indonesia. This picture shows a calm coastline before December 26, 2004

The tsunamis that struck the Indian Ocean in 2004 washed away everything in their way – roads, buildings, bridges and hundreds of thousands of people

Caught unawares

People who are unaware of the danger that accompanies a tsunami may often remain at the shore due to curiosity, or perhaps to collect fish when the sea withdraws before a tsunami. And when the tsunami strikes with all its force, it is often too late for them to run.

In Preparation

Earthquakes can strike any time, and foolproof warning systems are yet to be developed, so we must look to special building techniques and survival knowledge to protect ourselves.

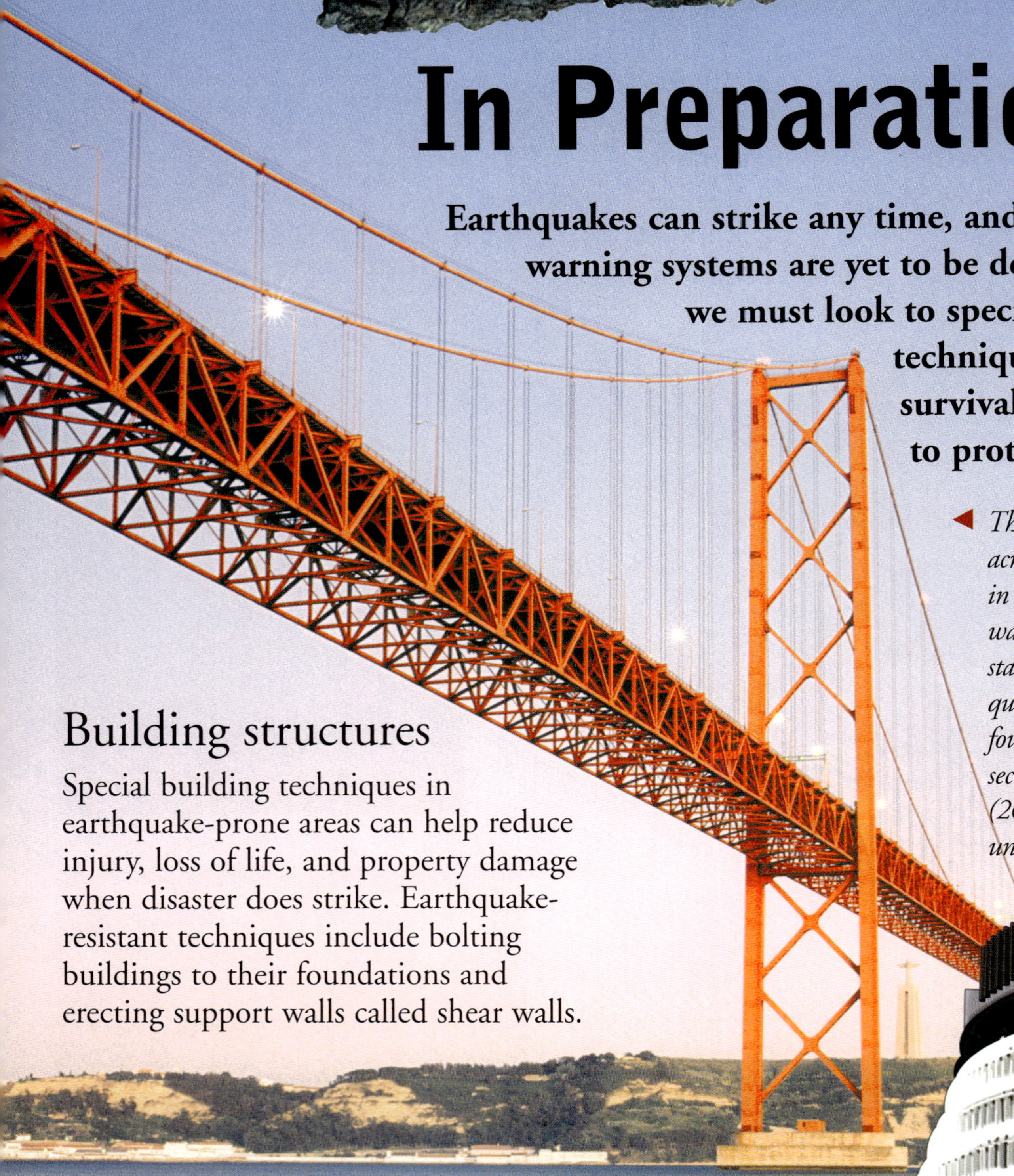

The suspension bridge across the Tagus River in Lisbon, Portugal, was designed to withstand major earthquakes. One of its foundations was secured 79 metres (260 feet) deep under the water

Building structures

Special building techniques in earthquake-prone areas can help reduce injury, loss of life, and property damage when disaster does strike. Earthquake-resistant techniques include bolting buildings to their foundations and erecting support walls called shear walls.

The Beehive Parliament House in New Zealand is just 400 metres (1,312 feet) from the Wellington fault zone, which is capable of causing big earthquakes. The building had to be rebuilt with new foundations, stronger walls and new beams. Specially made blocks of rubber and lead were placed between the foundations and the main beams

Fastened down

In earthquake-resistant homes, schools and workplaces, structures such as heavy appliances and furniture are fastened down to prevent them from falling over when the building shakes. Gas and water lines are purposefully laid with flexible joints to prevent leakage.

INTERESTING FACT

In the event of a major or even moderate earthquake, the frequency of aftershocks can go up to 1,000 or more in the course of a single day. Aftershocks can follow weeks and even months after the main earthquake.

FACT FILE

LARGEST EVACUATIONS BEFORE VOLCANIC ERUPTION

- **Nyiragongo, 2002:** About 500,000 evacuated in Congo
- **Pinatubo, 1991:** About 250,000 evacuated in the Philippines
- **Galunggung, 1982:** About 75,000 evacuated in Indonesia
- **Mayon, 1984:** About 73,000 evacuated in the Philippines

If stuck indoors during an earthquake, the best safety measure is to take cover under a piece of heavy furniture and hold on to it, or simply stand against an inside wall

The aftershocks

A large earthquake may be accompanied by many quakes of smaller magnitude. These later quakes are called after-shocks and can cause immense damage. The safe option is to steer clear of walls, windows, staircases and smashed structures that could crash.

Evacuation

Unlike earthquakes, a volcano eruption can be predicted more certainly. Once volcanologists warn of an eruption, the area around the volcano is evacuated. While damage to property cannot be avoided, lives can definitely be saved.

Rescue Mission

A rescue team waits for a building to be propped up, before entering. Buildings, weakened by earthquakes, can collapse well after the shock

Relief and rescue efforts must be put in operation immediately after the disaster strikes. Rescue workers look for survivors in the aftermath of an earthquake or a volcanic eruption.

Honeycombed in

Collapsed buildings are like honeycombs with void spaces, which allow those trapped inside to survive. In the instance of the 1992 Philippines earthquake, a man was extracted with a broken ankle after 13 days trapped in a hotel that had collapsed during the event.

Miracles

Often, unusual survival stories are termed as 'miracles'. The rescue team, however, know that such a possibility always exists. It has to be careful and patient while digging through the rubble.

People trapped in earthquake rubble stand a better chance of survival if they are rescued within 72 hours

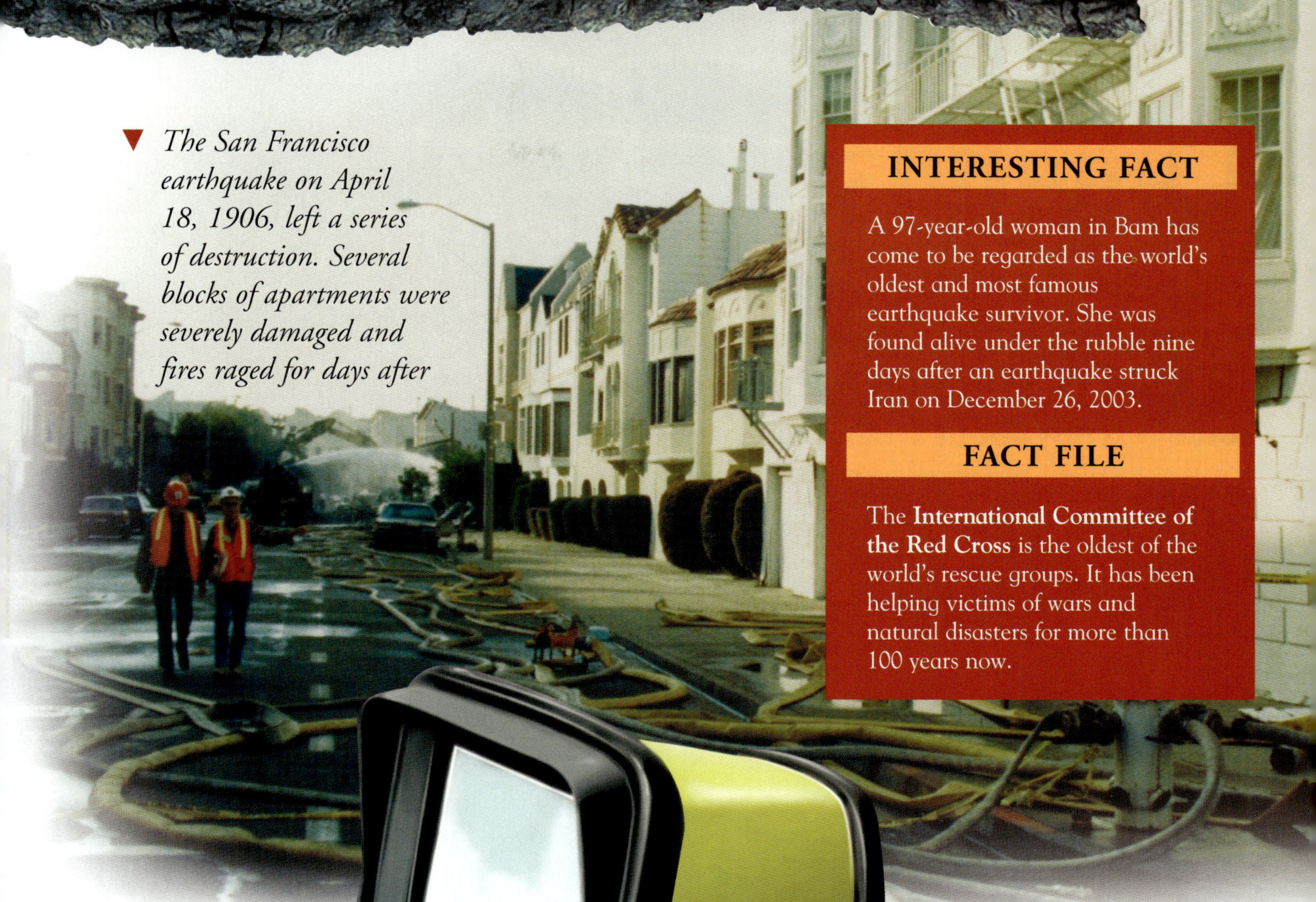

The San Francisco earthquake on April 18, 1906, left a series of destruction. Several blocks of apartments were severely damaged and fires raged for days after

INTERESTING FACT

A 97-year-old woman in Bam has come to be regarded as the world's oldest and most famous earthquake survivor. She was found alive under the rubble nine days after an earthquake struck Iran on December 26, 2003.

FACT FILE

The **International Committee of the Red Cross** is the oldest of the world's rescue groups. It has been helping victims of wars and natural disasters for more than 100 years now.

Hi-tech search

Firefighters use a range of customised devices to locate victims trapped within void spaces in collapsed structures. Such devices include fibre-optic and Ground Penetrating Radar technology, special search cameras, highly sensitive instruments for sensing sound and vibration, search dogs, and direct visual and voice contact.

Earthquake rescue teams use thermal-image cameras to locate survivors trapped in the rubble

Volcano rescue team

With volcano-watching becoming a favoured attraction for tourists, volcano rescue teams have been formed for any emergencies that may happen. These men are specially trained for rescue efforts on mountains.

Legends

Around the world, various people have tried to explain earthquakes and volcanoes in different ways. Here are some legends about what makes the ground shake and erupt!

According to Mexican legend, earthquakes are caused when the devil makes giant rips in the Earth from the inside!

Devilish moves

In Mexico, it was believed that El Diablo, the devil, made giant cuts in the Earth from the inside. Thus, he and his devilish mates could use the cracks to go up and carry out mischief on Earth whenever they wanted to.

Vulcan's forge

People in Sicily believed that the lava fragments and dust clouds erupting from a volcano came from the god Vulcan's forge as he cut out thunderbolts for Jupiter, king of the gods, and weapons for Mars, the god of war. Vulcan was the god of fire in Roman religion.

The word 'volcano' comes from the island of Vulcano, off Sicily. Centuries ago, people there believed that Vulcano was the chimney of the god Vulcan's forge

Baby Ru

A legend in New Zealand has it that Mother Earth carries within her womb a child, the young god Ru. And every time he stretches and kicks – as babies do – an earthquake happens!

INTERESTING FACT

Legend describes Pele, the goddess of fire in Hawaiian religion, as an expert rider of the holua, a wooden sled that skates down steep slopes. Once, Papalauahi and other chiefs challenged Pele to a competition to judge who the best holua rider was. Papalauahi won the race. Pele, who was noted for her anger, produced a great flood of lava that swept away several of the chiefs and bystanders, creating lava trees out of them!

FACT FILE

Central American folklore relates that the square Earth is kept hoisted at its four corners by four gods. When the gods believe the Earth is becoming too crowded, they tilt it to get rid of the extra people.

Hawaiian people attributed volcanic activity to the beautiful but wrathful Pele, the goddess of fire. Whenever she was angry or spiteful, she made volcanoes erupt with fire!

In the 4th century BC, Aristotle proposed that earthquakes were caused by winds trapped in caves under the ground

Greek idea

In Greece, the philosopher Aristotle proposed that strong, unruly winds are trapped in underground caverns. As these winds thrash about struggling to escape, earthquakes hit the Earth.

Fascinating Facts

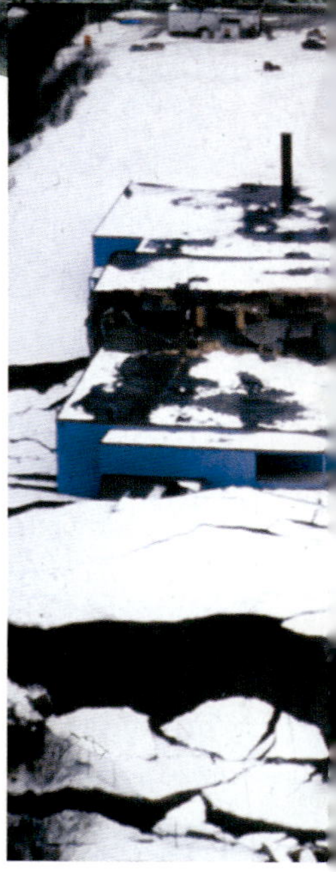

Volcanoes are nature's fireworks on display, while earthquakes occur when the Earth gets a bit shaken up. While both cause large-scale damage, they are nonetheless very fascinating. In fact, tourists are known to throng to volcanic areas in the hope of catching a glimpse of streaming lava or surging smoke.

Close quarters

Volcanologists have ventured into the craters of some volcanoes. But nobody really goes all the way down, since it is too hot and filled with poisonous gases. One can only learn about the way volcanoes work by looking down old craters.

▼ *Volcanologists have to sometimes explore inside a crater to collect rock and gas samples for study*

Moonquakes

Moonquakes (tremor on the Moon's surface) have been observed, but their frequency is less than of earthquakes. Also, moonquakes are much smaller in magnitude than the quakes on Earth. Most moonquakes occur at great depth, about halfway between the surface and the centre of the Moon.

► *Moonquakes were first discovered during the Apollo missions to the Moon. Moonquakes are much weaker than earthquakes, as the Moon's core is colder and has a solid mantle – unlike the Earth's molten core*

Alaska is one of the most earthquake-prone areas in the world, with over 4,000 earthquakes recorded at various depths in a year

INTERESTING FACT

Alaska is the most earthquake-prone state in the world. Earthquakes of magnitude 7 occur there almost every year, while those of magnitude 8 or bigger happen every 14 years on average.

FACT FILE

An **earthquake of magnitude 5** may release energy 10,000 times as much as that of the first atomic bomb

The animal sense

It is believed that animals can sense the onset of earthquakes, and that they start behaving strangely. Such changes in behaviour cannot, however, be used to predict earthquakes precisely, since a connection between a specific behaviour and the occurrence of an earthquake has not been made yet.

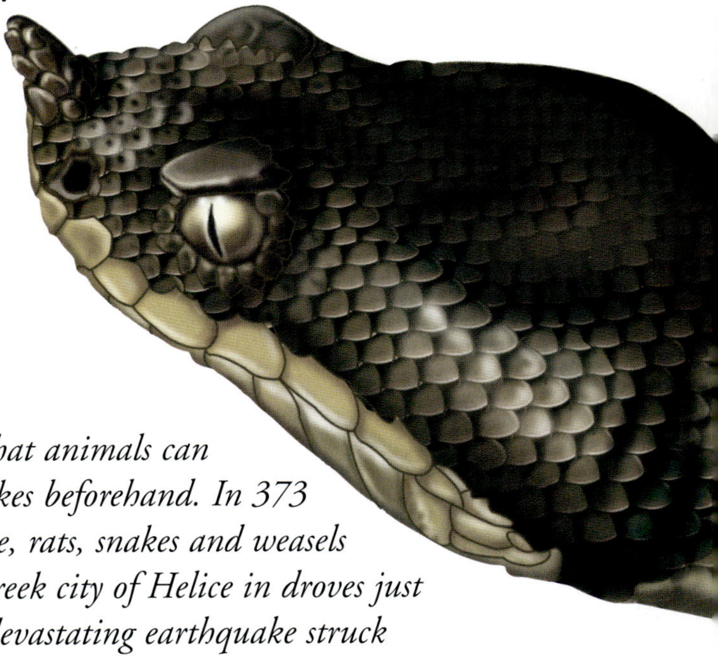

It is believed that animals can sense earthquakes beforehand. In 373 BC, for instance, rats, snakes and weasels deserted the Greek city of Helice in droves just days before a devastating earthquake struck

Manmade quakes

Human beings have also been responsible for causing earthquakes. The building-up of large masses of water behind dams, digging of mines, injection of fluid into the Earth's crust, and detonation of huge bombs are some human activities that can lead to earthquakes.

Glossary

Aerosol: Fine liquid or gas particles that are distributed through gas, usually air

Avalanche: Large mass of rock debris or snow that slides down a mountain slope rapidly and forcefully

Basalt: Volcanic rock that is dark in colour and usually dense and smooth

Black sand: Created by the interaction of hot lava with cold seawater, as a result of which the lava bubble bursts to form small crystals

Climate change: Long-term, major change recorded in the weather trends of an area

Conduit: Channel that conveys water or other fluid

Core: The extremely hot centre of the Earth, existing in a largely molten state; composed of a large quantity of iron

Debris: Collection of fragments of rock and other material

Detonation: An explosion, or the act of exploding

Dinosaur: Group of reptiles that first appeared about 215 million years ago and no longer exist

Evacuation: Shifting from a place of danger to one of greater safety

Fatality: Death brought on by an accident or a disaster

Fumarole: Volcanic vent that issues forth gas and steam

Geologist: Scientist who studies the origin, history, structure and composition of the Earth

Granite: Light-coloured, coarse igneous rock; formed by the cooling of magma under the Earth's crust

Gravity: The force of attraction that pulls bodies toward the centre of a celestial body, such as the Earth

Hotspot: Region inside the Earth marked by extreme heat and believed to be the site of active volcanic activity

Hot spring: Natural spring that produces water usually warmer than body temperature; formed mainly by the interaction of groundwater with either molten rock or hot igneous rock

Igneous rock: Formed when magma cools down and becomes solid

Landslide: Downward movement of a mass of rock or earth, along a slope

Lava: Molten rock (magma) that reaches the Earth's surface

Lunar: Relating to the Earth's Moon

Magma: Molten or partially molten rock found under the Earth's crust

Magma chamber: Underground reservoir, especially beneath a volcano, holding molten material

Magnitude: Measure of the amount of energy released during an earthquake; recorded on the Richter scale

Mid-ocean ridge: Series of mountain range at the ocean basin

NASA: National Aeronautics and Space Administration, an independent agency of the United States government for space research and travel

Observatory: A place equipped for studying astronomical, weather-related or other natural phenomena

Pillow lava: Volcanic lava hardened into an elongated, pillow-shaped formation; formed underwater

Pumice: Light, frothy volcanic rock formed from rapidly cooling lava that is full of gas

Pyroclastic: Rock or mineral fragment formed during a volcanic eruption

Radiation: Emission and transmission of energy in the form of rays and waves

Rheumatism: A variety of disorders of the muscles, joints or connective tissue

Seismic wave: Vibration caused through the Earth by an earthquake or explosion

Seismogram: Diagram of earthquake waves recorded by a seismograph

Seismograph: Instrument that records earthquake waves

Stress: The resisting force built up in a body due to an external force

Submarine: Below the surface of the sea

Tephra: Solid matter ejected into the air during a volcanic eruption

Tidal wave: A large wave along the seashore often caused by wind and high tide

Tiltmeter: Instrument to measure the expansion of a volcano by tracking the rising or lowering of magma levels

Toxic: Capable of causing health problem or even death, particularly by chemicals

Tsunami: Very large ocean wave usually caused by an underwater earthquake, and occasionally by submarine landslides and volcanic eruptions